COOKING ON A BUDGET
family meals

COOKING ON A BUDGET
family meals
easy to buy, prepare and cook

p

This is a Parragon Book
First Published in 2005

Parragon
Queen Street House
4 Queen Street
Bath BA1 1HE
United Kingdom

This edition designed by Fiona Roberts.
Photography and text by The Bridgewater Book Company Ltd.

ISBN: 1-40544-883-0

Printed in China

NOTE
This book uses metric and imperial measurements. Follow the same units of measurement
throughout; do not mix metric and imperial. All spoon measurements are level: teaspoons are
assumed to be 5 ml and tablespoons are assumed to be 15 ml. Unless otherwise stated, milk
is assumed to be full fat, eggs and individual vegetables such as potatoes are medium, and
pepper is freshly ground black pepper.

The times given for each recipe are an approximate guide only because the preparation times
may differ accordingly to the techniques used by different people and the cooking times may
vary as a result of the type of oven and other equipment used.

Recipes using raw or very lightly cooked eggs should be avoided by infants, the elderly,
pregnant women, convalescents and anyone suffering from an illness. Pregnant
and breast-feeding women are advised to avoid eating peanuts and peanut products.

contents

introduction   **page 6**

soups, snacks & sides   **p10**
Tomato Soup   p12
Cream of Chicken Soup   p14
Cheesy Vegetable Chowder   p16
Carrot & Cumin Soup   p18
Pea & Ham Soup   p19
Potato Crumble   p20
Tomato & Onion Bake   p22
Spanish Potato Omelette   p24
Cheese & Potato Slices   p26
Pan-Fried Liver & Bacon
   with Potato Cakes   p27
Bubble & Squeak   p28
Bread & Butter Savoury   p30

Chilli Beans   p32
Paprika Potatoes   p34
Crispy Vegetable Pancakes   p35
Herby Potatoes & Onion   p36

main meals   **p38**
Spaghetti Bolognese   p40
Beef in Beer with Herb
   Dumplings   p42
Beef & Tomato Gratin   p44
Spaghetti & Meatballs   p45
Chilli con Carne   p46
Carrot-Topped Beef Pie   p48
Shepherd's Pie   p50
Lamb & Potato Moussaka   p52
Pasticcio   p53

Pork Hash   p54
Chicken Bake   p56
Chicken Pepperonata   p58
Jamaican Hot Pot   p60
Minty Lime Chicken   p61
Macaroni & Tuna Fish Layer p62
Smoked Fish Lasagne   p64
Spaghetti alla Puttanesca   p66
Spaghettini with Quick
   Tuna Sauce   p68
Potato & Vegetable Curry   p69
Vegetable Enchiladas   p70
Tomato, Mushroom &
   Macaroni Hot Pot   p72
Cold Weather Casserole   p74
Mushroom & Bean Chilli   p76

Chickpea Hot Pot   p77
Vegetable Crumble   p78
Vegetable & Lentil Casserole p80

desserts   **p82**
Chocolate Fudge Pudding   p84
Queen of Puddings   p86
Bread & Butter Pudding   p87
Traditional Apple Pie   p88
Fruit Brûlée   p90
Lemon Meringue Pie   p92
Pear Cake   p94
Chocolate Fruit Crumble   p95

index   **p96**

introduction

Our mothers and grandmothers, who often raised larger families than those of today, knew a thing or two about how to prepare tasty, wholesome and filling meals on a tight budget. Nowadays we are pressured not only by a shortage of time, but also by advertising, so it is all too easy to resort to ready-made products. This is an expensive way to feed a family and is nothing like delicious and healthy home-cooked meals.

Fresh is not just best, it is more flavoursome and nutritious and it doesn't have to be expensive. When buying fruit and vegetables think seasonal. Strawberries in the mid-winter might seem like a treat, but they are often disappointingly tasteless and absurdly priced, whereas home-grown apples are in season, delicious and inexpensive. The less expensive cuts of meat, such as braising steak, are often the ones with most flavour - they just require longer, slower cooking, but this results in tender and succulent casseroles, stews and curries. What's more, these kinds of dishes are incredibly easy to prepare.

Shopping

Plan the week's menus before you go shopping, write a list and stick to it. Bear in mind that supermarkets take great care to display their products to tempt customers to buy more than they need and to choose the more expensive brands. You may not be aware that to reach staples, such as flour, rice and pasta, you will have to push your trolley past eye-catching shelves stacked with colourfully packaged biscuits, crisps and jars of ready-made sauces. The more expensive brands are usually displayed on shelves at eye level, while the cheaper varieties are placed lower down.

There are bargains to be had, but think twice before you put the 'two for the price of one' or '15 per cent extra' packet in your basket. Check the 'use-by' date as it's no bargain if you end up throwing half of it away. Nor is it value for money if it's not something the family is going to like. Nevertheless, such special offers can extend the budget if they apply to things you know you will use, especially if you can store them in the freezer.

Money-saving tips

■ Allow plenty of time for shopping rather than having to make a harassed dash around the supermarket on a Friday evening and, if you can, leave the kids at home.

BUDGETING GUIDE	
£	Bargain
££	Budget
£££	Economical

■ Don't go shopping on an empty stomach as you are more likely to be tempted to buy things you don't really need.

■ If you are going to heat up the oven for one dish, save energy and therefore money by adding another - a

There are hundreds of dishes to make using the simplest of ingredients

main course casserole and a pie for dessert. Cook ahead for tomorrow while cooking tonight's dinner or bake in batches.

■ Steaming is a great way to cook green vegetables and you can save energy by cooking one thing on top of another.

■ If a recipe requires chicken portions, buy a whole chicken and cut it into pieces with a heavy knife or cleaver.

■ Fresh herbs are fabulous for adding flavour to all kinds of dishes and are much less

Fabulous family meals can be created without great expense

expensive than ready-made sauces. If you can grow them in your garden, in a window-box or in pots the kitchen, they are virtually free and truly fresh.

■ Make your own stock and freeze it in ice cube trays - it keeps for up to six months. You can add one or two cubes whenever stock is required and this is much cheaper, tastier and probably healthier than using bouillon powder or stock cubes.

■ Save the carcasses and bones from roast chicken for making stock. Store them in a plastic bag in the freezer until you have enough for the recipe (see page 9).

■ Peel potatoes after boiling them (scrub them first). Not only will there be less waste, but more vitamins will be retained.

■ Make the most of cheap-and-cheerful fillers, such as pasta, rice, potatoes, pulses, pastry and dumplings.

basic chicken stock

- makes 2.5 litres/4½ pints
- preparation time: 10 minutes, plus chilling
- cooking time: 3¼ hours

1.25 kg/2 lb 12 oz chicken and/or
turkey wings, necks and backs
or 4 carcasses and bones from
whole roast chickens
2 onions, quartered
2 celery sticks, coarsely chopped
2 carrots, coarsely chopped

4 fresh parsley sprigs
2 fresh thyme sprigs
1 bay leaf
8 black peppercorns, coarsely
crushed

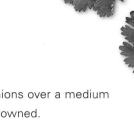

1 Heat the oil in a large saucepan and cook the chicken or turkey and onions over a medium heat, stirring and turning occasionally, for 10-15 minutes until lightly browned.

2 Pour in 4 litres/7 pints water and stir well, scraping up any sediment from the base of the pan. Bring to the boil and skim off any scum that rises to the surface. Add all the remaining ingredients, lower the heat, cover and simmer for 3 hours.

3 Strain the stock into a bowl, leave to cool, then chill in the refrigerator. When the stock is cold, remove the layer of fat that has formed on the surface.

soups, snacks & sides

Serve the delicious dishes in this chapter as starters and light meals

or as filling accompaniments without breaking the bank.

Home-made soup is always a welcome treat, while other favourites

include Spanish Potato Omelette, Bubble & Squeak,

Chilli Beans and Crispy Vegetable Pancakes.

£€ tomato soup

- serves 4
- prepared in 10 mins
- cooks in 25 mins

55 g/2 oz butter

1 onion, finely chopped

700 g/1 lb 9 oz tomatoes, finely chopped

salt and pepper

600 ml/1 pint hot chicken or vegetable stock (see page 9)

pinch of sugar

100 ml/3½ fl oz single cream

2 tbsp shredded fresh basil leaves

1 tbsp chopped fresh parsley

1 Melt half the butter in a large, heavy-based saucepan. Add the onion and cook over a low heat, stirring occasionally, for 5 minutes, or until softened. Add the tomatoes, season to taste with salt and pepper and cook for 5 minutes.

2 Pour in the hot chicken or vegetable stock, return to the boil, then reduce the heat and cook for 10 minutes.

3 Push the soup through a sieve with the back of a wooden spoon to remove the tomato skins and seeds. Return to the saucepan and stir in the sugar, cream, remaining butter, basil and parsley. Heat through briefly, but do not allow to boil. Ladle into warmed soup bowls and serve immediately.

1   2   3

cream of chicken soup

£££

- serves 4
- prepared in 15 mins + 10 mins to cool
- cooks in 40 mins

3 tbsp butter

4 shallots, chopped

1 leek, trimmed and sliced

450 g/1 lb skinless chicken
breasts, chopped

600 ml/1 pint chicken stock

1 tbsp chopped fresh parsley

1 tbsp chopped fresh thyme

salt and pepper

175 ml/6 fl oz double cream

sprigs of fresh thyme,
  to garnish

fresh crusty rolls, to serve

1 Melt the butter in a large saucepan over a medium heat. Add the shallots and cook, stirring, for 3 minutes, until slightly softened. Add the leek and cook for a further 5 minutes, stirring. Add the chicken, stock and herbs, and season with salt and pepper. Bring to the boil, then lower the heat and simmer for 25 minutes, until the chicken is tender and cooked through. Remove from the heat and leave to cool for 10 minutes.

2 Transfer the soup into a food processor and blend until smooth (you may need to do this in batches). Return the soup to the pan and warm over a low heat for 5 minutes.

3 Stir in the cream and cook for a further 2 minutes, then remove from the heat and ladle into serving bowls. Garnish with sprigs of thyme and serve with fresh crusty rolls.

cheesy vegetable chowder

££

- serves 4
- prepared in 15 mins
- cooks in 45 mins

25 g/1 oz butter

1 large onion, finely chopped

1 large leek, split lengthways
   and thinly sliced

1-2 garlic cloves, crushed

55 g/2 oz plain flour

1.2 litres/2 pints vegetable stock

3 carrots, finely diced

2 celery sticks, finely diced

1 turnip, finely diced

1 large potato, finely diced

3–4 sprigs fresh thyme or ⅛ tsp
   dried thyme

1 bay leaf

350 ml/12 fl oz single cream

300 g/10½ oz mature Cheddar
   cheese, grated

salt and pepper

chopped fresh parsley,
   to garnish

1 Melt the butter in a large heavy-based saucepan over a low-medium heat. Add the onion, leek and garlic. Cover and cook for about 5 minutes, stirring frequently, until the vegetables are starting to soften.

2 Stir the flour into the vegetables and continue cooking for 2 minutes. Add a little of the stock and stir well, scraping the bottom of the pan to mix in the flour. Bring to the boil, stirring frequently, and slowly stir in the rest of the stock.

3 Add the carrots, celery, turnip, potato, thyme and bay leaf. Reduce the heat, cover the pan and cook the soup gently for about 35 minutes, stirring occasionally, until the vegetables are tender. Remove the bay leaf and the thyme sprigs.

4 Stir in the cream and simmer over a very low heat for 5 minutes.

5 Add the cheese a handful at a time, stirring constantly for 1 minute after each addition to make sure it is completely melted. Do not boil. Taste the soup and adjust the seasoning, adding salt if needed, and pepper to taste.

6 Ladle the soup immediately into warm bowls, sprinkle with chopped fresh parsley and serve.

2   3   5

carrot & cumin soup

- serves 4 - 6
- prepared in 15 mins
- cooks in 45 mins

3 tbsp butter or margarine

1 large onion, chopped

1–2 garlic cloves, crushed

350 g/12 oz carrots, sliced

900 ml/1½ pints vegetable
   stock

¾ tsp ground cumin

salt and pepper

2 celery sticks, thinly sliced

115 g/4 oz potato, diced

2 tsp tomato purée

2 tsp lemon juice

2 bay leaves

about 300 ml/½ pint
   skimmed milk

celery leaves, to garnish

1 Melt the butter or margarine in a large pan. Add the onion and garlic and cook very gently until softened.

2 Add the carrots and cook gently for a further 5 minutes, stirring frequently and taking care they do not brown.

3 Add the stock, cumin, seasoning, celery, potato, tomato purée, lemon juice and bay leaves and bring to the boil. Cover and simmer for about 30 minutes until the vegetables are tender.

4 Remove and discard the bay leaves, cool the soup a little and then press it through a sieve or process in a food processor or blender until smooth.

5 Pour the soup into a clean pan, add the milk and bring to the boil over a low heat. Taste and adjust the seasoning if necessary.

6 Ladle the soup into warmed bowls, garnish each serving with a small celery leaf and serve.

pea & ham soup

£££

- serves 4
- prepared in 10 mins + 10 mins to cool
- cooks in 45 mins

1 tbsp butter

1 onion, sliced

1 leek, trimmed and sliced

1 litre/1¾ pints vegetable stock

450 g/1 lb freshly shelled
peas, or frozen peas, defrosted

200 g/7 oz lean smoked ham,
chopped

1 bay leaf

1 tbsp chopped fresh tarragon

salt and pepper

4 tbsp double cream

cooked ham, chopped

sprigs of fresh tarragon
to garnish

fresh crusty rolls, to serve

1 Melt the butter in a large saucepan over a medium heat. Add the onion and cook, stirring, for 3 minutes, until slightly softened. Add the leek and cook for a further 2 minutes, stirring. Stir in the stock, then add the peas, ham, bay leaf and tarragon. Season with salt and pepper. Bring to the boil, then lower the heat and simmer for 30 minutes. Remove from the heat and discard the bay leaf. Leave to cool for 10 minutes.

2 Transfer half of the soup into a food processor and blend until smooth. Return to the pan with the rest of the soup, stir in the cream and cook over a low heat for a further 5 minutes.

3 Remove the soup from the heat and ladle into serving bowls. Garnish with chopped ham and sprigs of fresh tarragon and serve with fresh crusty rolls.

potato crumble

- serves 4
- prepared in 25 mins
- cooks in 30 mins

900g/2lb floury potatoes, diced
25 g/1 oz butter
2 tbsp milk
50 g/1¾ oz mature Cheddar
  cheese or blue cheese, grated
CRUMBLE TOPPING
40 g/1½ oz butter
1 onion, cut into chunks
1 garlic clove, crushed
1 tbsp wholegrain mustard
175 g/6 oz fresh wholemeal
  breadcrumbs
2 tbsp chopped fresh parsley
salt and pepper

1 Cook the potatoes in a pan of lightly salted boiling water for 10 minutes, or until cooked through.

2 Meanwhile, make the crumble topping. Melt the butter in a frying pan. Add the onion, garlic and mustard and fry over a medium heat, stirring constantly, for 5 minutes, until the onion has softened.

3 Put the breadcrumbs in a mixing bowl and stir in the fried onion mixture and chopped parsley. Season to taste with salt and pepper.

4 Drain the potatoes thoroughly and place them in another mixing bowl. Add the butter and milk, then mash until smooth. Stir in the grated cheese while the potato is still hot.

5 Spoon the mashed potato into a shallow ovenproof dish and sprinkle with the crumble topping.

6 Cook the potato crumble in a preheated oven, 200°C/400°F/Gas Mark 6, for 10–15 minutes, until the topping is golden brown and crunchy. Serve immediately.

2   4   5

tomato & onion bake

£

- serves 4
- prepared in 10 mins
- cooks in 1 hour

55 g/2 oz butter, plus extra for greasing
2 large onions, thinly sliced
500 g/1 lb 2 oz tomatoes,
  skinned and sliced
115 g/4 oz fresh white breadcrumbs
  salt and pepper
4 eggs

2

1 Grease an ovenproof dish with butter. Melt 40 g/1½ oz of the butter in a heavy-based frying pan. Add the onions and cook over a low heat, stirring occasionally, for 5 minutes, until softened.

2 Layer the onions, tomatoes and breadcrumbs in the dish, seasoning each layer with salt and pepper to taste. Dot the remaining butter on top and bake in a preheated oven, 180°C/350°F/ Gas Mark 4, for 40 minutes.

2

3 Make 4 hollows in the mixture with the back of a spoon. Crack 1 egg into each hollow. Return the dish to the oven and bake for 15 minutes more, until the eggs are just set. Serve immediately.

3

spanish potato omelette

- serves 6
- prepared in 20 mins
- cooks in 35 mins

125 ml/4 fl oz olive oil
600 g/1 lb 5 oz potatoes, sliced
1 large onion, sliced
1 large garlic clove, crushed
6 large eggs
salt and pepper

1 Heat a 25 cm/10 inch frying pan, preferably non-stick, over a high heat. Pour in the olive oil and heat. Lower the heat, add the potatoes, onion and garlic and cook for 15–20 minutes, stirring frequently, until the potatoes are tender.

2 Beat the eggs together in a large bowl and season generously with salt and pepper. Using a slotted spoon, transfer the potatoes and onion to the bowl of eggs. Pour the excess oil left in the frying pan into a heatproof jug, then scrape off the crusty bits from the base of the pan.

3 Reheat the pan and add about 2 tablespoons of the oil reserved in the jug. Pour in the potato mixture, smoothing the vegetables into an even layer. Cook for about 5 minutes, shaking the pan occasionally, or until the base is set.

4 Shake the pan and use a spatula to loosen the edge of the omelette. Place a large plate over the pan. Carefully invert the omelette on to the plate.

5 If you are not using a non-stick pan, add 1 tablespoon of the reserved oil to the pan and swirl around. Gently slide the omelette back into the pan, cooked-side up. Use the spatula to 'tuck down' the edge of the omelette. Continue cooking over medium heat for 3–5 minutes until set.

6 Remove the pan from the heat and slide the tortilla on to a serving plate. Leave to stand for at least 5 minutes before cutting. Serve hot, warm or at room temperature with salad.

1

3

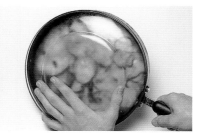

4

££

cheese & potato slices

- serves 4
- prepared in 10 mins
- cooks in 40 mins

900 g/2 lb waxy potatoes,
    unpeeled and thickly sliced
70 g/2½ oz fresh white
    breadcrumbs
40 g/1½ oz Parmesan
    cheese, freshly grated
1½ tsp chilli powder
2 eggs, beaten

oil, for deep frying
chilli powder, for dusting
    (optional)

1 Cook the potatoes in a saucepan of boiling water for about 10–15 minutes, or until the
potatoes are just tender. Drain thoroughly.

2 Mix the breadcrumbs, cheese and chilli powder together in a bowl, then transfer to a shallow
dish. Pour the beaten eggs into a separate shallow dish.

3 Dip the potato slices first in egg and then roll them in the breadcrumbs to coat completely.

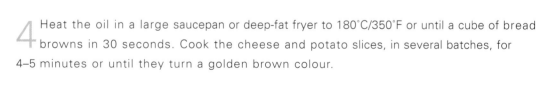

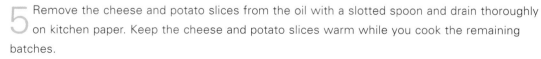

4 Heat the oil in a large saucepan or deep-fat fryer to 180°C/350°F or until a cube of bread
browns in 30 seconds. Cook the cheese and potato slices, in several batches, for
4–5 minutes or until they turn a golden brown colour.

5 Remove the cheese and potato slices from the oil with a slotted spoon and drain thoroughly
on kitchen paper. Keep the cheese and potato slices warm while you cook the remaining
batches.

6 Transfer the cheese and potato slices to warm individual serving plates. Dust lightly with
chilli powder, if using, and serve immediately.

NOTE: If you invest in a block of fresh Parmesan it can be stored in the fridge for a long period and
thus becomes an economical ingredient.

pan-fried liver & bacon with potato cakes

££

- serves 4
- prepared in 20 mins
- cooks in 20 - 30 mins

450 g/1 lb potatoes, peeled
1 egg, beaten
4 tbsp plain white flour, plus
**   extra for dusting**
salt and pepper
450 g/1 lb sliced lamb's liver
sunflower oil, for frying
4 bacon rashers
2 onions, sliced finely

1 Grate the potatoes, then rinse under cold running water until the water runs clear. Squeeze out the water and dry the potatoes in a clean tea towel. Put the potatoes in a large bowl and add the egg, flour, salt and pepper and mix well together. Dust the liver with flour and add salt and pepper.

2 Heat about 5 mm/¼ inch oil in a large frying pan, then add large tablespoons of the potato mixture, flattening them with a spatula. Cook for about 10 minutes, turning once, until golden brown. Remove from the pan and keep hot. Continue until all the mixture has been cooked.

1

3 Meanwhile, in a separate frying pan, heat enough oil to cover the base. Add the bacon and fry until crisp, then push to one side of the pan. Add the onions and cook for 5 minutes, or until browned. Push to one side of the pan, add the liver and fry for 6–8 minutes, turning once, until tender. Serve with the potato cakes.

1

2

bubble & squeak

■ serves 4
■ prepared in 15 mins
■ cooks in 1 hour

450 g/1 lb potatoes, unpeeled

70 g/2½ oz butter

salt and pepper

225 g/8 oz cabbage

2–3 tbsp water

4 tbsp sunflower oil

1 onion, finely chopped

1 Cook the potatoes in lightly salted boiling water for 25 minutes, or until tender. Drain and peel, then dice. Place the potatoes in a large bowl with 55 g/2 oz of the butter and mash until no lumps remain. Season to taste with salt and pepper. Meanwhile, shred the cabbage, place it in a large, heavy-based saucepan and add the remaining butter and the water. Cover and cook over a low heat, shaking the saucepan occasionally, for 10 minutes, or until tender.

2 Mix the cabbage and mashed potato together in a bowl and season to taste with salt and pepper. Heat half the oil in a heavy-based frying pan. Add the onion and cook, stirring occasionally, for 5 minutes, or until softened. Add the potato and cabbage mixture and press down with the back of a wooden spoon to make a flat, even cake.

3 Cook over a medium heat for 15 minutes, until the underside is golden brown. Invert the vegetable cake on to a large plate. Add the remaining oil to the frying pan. Return the cake to the frying pan to cook the other side. Cook for 10 minutes, or until the second side is golden brown. Transfer to a plate, cut into wedges and serve.

1   1   2

bread & butter savoury

£

- serves 4
- prepared in 30 mins
- cooks in 45 mins

60 g/2 oz butter or margarine
1 bunch spring onions, sliced
6 slices of white or brown
   bread, crusts removed
175g/6 oz mature Cheddar
   cheese, grated
2 eggs
450 ml/16 fl oz milk

salt and pepper
fresh flat-leaf parsley sprigs,
to garnish

3

4

5

1 Lightly grease a 1.5 litre/2½ pint ovenproof dish with a little of the butter or margarine.

2 Melt the remaining butter or margarine in a small saucepan. Add the spring onions and fry over a medium heat, stirring occasionally, until softened and golden.

3 Meanwhile, cut the bread into triangles and place half of them in the base of the dish. Cover with the sliced spring onions and top with half the grated Cheddar cheese.

4 Beat together the eggs and milk and season to taste with salt and pepper. Layer the remaining triangles of bread in the dish and carefully pour over the milk mixture. Leave to soak for 15–20 minutes.

5 Sprinkle the remaining cheese over the soaked bread. Bake in a preheated oven, 190°C/375°F/Gas Mark 5, for 35–40 minutes, until puffed up and golden brown. Garnish with flat-leaf parsley and serve immediately.

chilli beans

- serves 4-6
- prepared in 10 mins + 8 hrs soaking
- cooks in 1 hr 20 mins

**200 g/7 oz dried mixed beans,
   such as kidney, soya, pinto,
   cannellini and chickpeas
1 red onion, diced
1 garlic clove, crushed
1 tbsp hot chilli powder
400 g/14 oz canned chopped
   tomatoes in tomato juice
1 tbsp tomato purée
4 tbsp low-fat natural yogurt
jacket potatoes, boiled rice
   or soft flour tortilla wraps,
   to serve**

1 Soak the beans overnight or for 8 hours in a large bowl of cold water. Drain, rinse and put the beans into a large saucepan. Cover well with cold water, then bring to the boil and boil rapidly for 10 minutes. Reduce the heat, cover and simmer for a further 45 minutes, or until tender. Drain. (Alternatively, if time is short, use 450 g/1 lb drained and rinsed canned mixed beans and start at Step 2.)

2 Put the cooked beans, onion, garlic, chilli powder, tomatoes and tomato purée into a saucepan and bring to the boil. Reduce the heat, cover and simmer for 20–25 minutes, or until the onion is tender.

3 Serve each portion of the chilli beans with a tablespoon of the yogurt, accompanied by jacket potatoes, boiled rice or soft flour tortilla wraps.

1   2   2

£

paprika potatoes

■ serves 4
■ prepared in 15 mins
■ cooks in 1 hour 10 mins

4 baking potatoes
125 ml/4 fl oz vegetable stock
1 onion, finely chopped
1 garlic clove, finely chopped
125 ml/4 fl oz natural yogurt
2 tsp paprika
salt and pepper

1

1 Prick the potatoes with a fork and bake in a preheated oven, 200°C/ 400°F/Gas Mark 6, for about 1 hour, until tender.

2 Just before the potatoes are ready, pour the stock into a saucepan and add the onion and garlic. Bring to the boil and simmer for 5 minutes.

3 Remove the potatoes from the oven and cut a lengthways slice from the top of each. Do not switch off the oven. Using a teaspoon, carefully scoop out the flesh, leaving a shell. Stir the potato flesh into the onion mixture, then add half the yogurt and 1 1/2 teaspoons of the paprika and season to taste with salt and pepper. Mix well and push through a sieve with the back of a wooden spoon.

4 Spoon the potato mixture into the potato shells and return to the oven for 10 minutes, until heated through. Top the potatoes with the remaining yogurt, sprinkle the remaining paprika over it and serve immediately.

3

4

crispy vegetable pancakes

£

- serves 4
- prepared in 10 mins
- cooks in 20 mins

2 large waxy potatoes

2 medium courgettes

1 egg, beaten

115 g/4 oz breadcrumbs

salt and pepper

oil for shallow frying

1 Peel and grate the potatoes. Turn into a sieve and drain out all the water and starch, pressing down hard. Remove the tops and bottoms from the courgettes and grate into a large bowl.

2 Combine the grated potatoes with the courgettes. Mix the egg and breadcrumbs into the vegetables and season with salt and pepper to taste.

3 Heat the oil in a large frying pan. Drop spoonfuls of the vegetable mixture into the hot oil and press down gently to make pancakes.

4 Fry the pancakes over a high heat for 5–10 minutes (depending on their thickness), until the bottom is golden brown and crispy. Turn and cook until the second side is brown and crispy. Lift out gently, drain on kitchen paper, place on a serving dish and keep warm until all the pancakes are cooked. Serve at once.

1

2

3

herby potatoes & onion

- serves 4
- prepared in 10 mins
- cooks in 50 mins

900 g/2 lb waxy potatoes,
  cut into cubes

125 g/4½ oz butter

1 red onion, cut into 8

2 garlic cloves, crushed

1 tsp lemon juice

2 tbsp chopped thyme

salt and pepper

1 Cook the cubed potatoes in a saucepan of boiling water for 10 minutes. Drain thoroughly.

2 Melt the butter in a large, heavy-based frying pan and add the red onion wedges, garlic and lemon juice. Cook, stirring constantly for 2–3 minutes.

3 Add the potatoes to the pan and mix well to coat in the butter mixture.

4 Reduce the heat, cover and cook for 25–30 minutes, or until the potatoes are golden brown and tender.

5 Sprinkle the chopped thyme over the top of the potatoes and season.

6 Transfer to a warm serving dish and serve immediately.

2   3   5

main meals

This fabulous collection of mouthwatering recipes is clear proof that you can eat well without spending the earth. Whether your taste is for pasta, pies, casseroles, curries or bakes, you are sure to find just the right dish for you and the family. Meat, poultry, fish and vegetables all play starring roles at reasonable prices.

spaghetti bolognese

€€€

- serves 4
- prepared in 1 hour 5 mins
- cooks in 20 mins

1 tbsp olive oil

1 onion, finely chopped

2 garlic cloves, chopped

1 carrot, scraped and chopped

1 stick celery, chopped

50 g/1¾ oz pancetta or streaky
    bacon, diced

350 g/12 oz lean minced beef

400 g/14 oz can chopped tomatoes

2 tsp dried oregano

125 ml/4 fl oz red wine

2 tbsp tomato purée

salt and pepper

675 g/1½ lb fresh spaghetti
    or 350 g/12 oz dried spaghetti

2

3

4

1 Heat the oil in a large frying pan. Add the onions and cook for 3 minutes.

2 Add the garlic, carrot, celery and pancetta or bacon and sauté for 3–4 minutes or until just beginning to brown.

3 Add the beef and cook over a high heat for another 3 minutes or until all of the meat is brown.

4 Stir in the tomatoes, oregano and red wine and bring to the boil. Reduce the heat and leave to simmer for about 45 minutes.

5 Stir in the tomato purée and season with salt and pepper.

6 Cook the spaghetti in a pan of boiling water for 8–10 minutes until tender, but still has 'bite'. Drain thoroughly.

7 Transfer the spaghetti to a serving plate and pour over the bolognese sauce. Toss to mix well and serve hot.

beef in beer with herb dumplings

(£££)

- serves 6
- prepared in 25 mins
- cooks in 2 hours 30 mins

STEW
2 tbsp sunflower oil
2 large onions, thinly sliced
8 carrots, sliced
4 tbsp plain flour
salt and pepper
1.25 kg/2 lb 12 oz stewing
    steak, cut into cubes
425 ml/15 fl oz stout
2 tsp muscovado sugar
2 bay leaves
1 tbsp chopped fresh thyme
HERB DUMPLINGS
115 g/4 oz self-raising flour
pinch of salt
55 g/2 oz shredded suet
2 tbsp chopped fresh parsley,
    plus extra to garnish
about 4 tbsp water

1 Preheat the oven to 160°C/
325°F/Gas Mark 3. Heat the
oil in a flameproof casserole.
Add the onions and carrots and
cook over a low heat, stirring
occasionally, for 5 minutes, or
until the onions are softened.
Meanwhile, place the flour in a
polythene bag and season with
salt and pepper. Add the stewing
steak to the bag, tie the top and
shake well to coat. Do this in
batches, if necessary.

2 Remove the vegetables from
the casserole with a slotted
spoon and reserve. Add the
stewing steak to the casserole,
in batches, and cook, stirring
frequently, until browned all over.

Return all the meat and the
onions and carrots to the casserole
and sprinkle in any remaining
seasoned flour. Pour in the stout
and add the sugar, bay leaves and
thyme. Bring to the boil, cover and
transfer to the preheated oven to
bake for 1 3/4 hours.

3 To make the herb dumplings,
sift the flour and salt into a
bowl. Stir in the suet and parsley
and add enough of the water to
make a soft dough. Shape into
small balls between the palms of
your hands. Add to the casserole
and return to the oven for 30
minutes. Remove and discard the
bay leaves. Serve immediately,
sprinkled with chopped parsley.

1   2   3

beef & tomato gratin

- serves 4
- prepared in 10 mins
- cooks in 1 hour 15 mins

350 g/12 oz lean beef mince
1 large onion, finely chopped
1 tsp dried mixed herbs
1 tbsp plain flour
300 ml/10 fl oz beef stock
1 tbsp tomato purée
salt and pepper

2 large tomatoes, thinly
   sliced
4 courgettes, thinly sliced
2 tbsp cornflour
300 ml/10 fl oz skimmed
   milk
150 ml/5 fl oz low-fat
   fromage frais

1 egg yolk
70 g/2½ oz freshly grated
   Parmesan cheese
crusty bread and steamed
   vegetables, to serve

1 Preheat the oven to 190°C/375°F/Gas Mark 5. In a large, heavy-based frying pan, dry-fry the beef and onion over a low heat, stirring frequently, for 4–5 minutes, or until the meat is browned all over. Stir in the dried mixed herbs, flour, beef stock and tomato purée and season to taste with salt and pepper. Bring to the boil, reduce the heat and simmer gently for 30 minutes, or until the mixture has thickened.

2 Transfer the mixture to an ovenproof gratin dish. Cover with a layer of the sliced tomatoes, then add a layer of sliced courgettes. Blend the cornflour with a little milk to make a smooth paste. Pour the remaining milk into a saucepan and bring to the boil. Add the cornflour mixture and cook, stirring, for 1–2 minutes, until thickened. Remove from the heat and beat in the fromage frais and egg yolk. Season to taste with salt and pepper.

3 Spread the white sauce over the layer of courgettes. Place the dish on a baking sheet and sprinkle with grated Parmesan cheese. Bake in the preheated oven for 25–30 minutes, or until the topping is golden brown and bubbling. Serve with crusty bread and steamed vegetables.

NOTE: If you invest in a block of fresh Parmesan it can be stored in the fridge for a long period and thus becomes an economical ingredient.

spaghetti & meatballs

££

- serves 6
- prepared in 20 mins, plus 30 mins chilling
- cooks in 45 mins

25 g/1 oz white bread, crusts removed and torn into pieces

2 tbsp milk

450 g/1 lb fresh beef mince

4 tbsp chopped fresh flat-leaf parsley

1 egg

pinch of cayenne pepper

salt and pepper

2 tbsp olive oil

150 ml/5 fl oz passata

200 g/7 oz canned chopped tomatoes

400 ml/14 fl oz vegetable stock

pinch of sugar

450 g/1 lb dried spaghetti

Place the bread in a small bowl, add the milk and leave to soak. Meanwhile, place the beef in a large bowl and add half the parsley, the egg and the cayenne pepper. Season to taste with salt and pepper. Squeeze the excess moisture out of the bread and crumble it over the meat mixture. Mix well until smooth.

Form small pieces of the mixture into balls between the palms of your hands and place on a tray or board. Leave to chill in the refrigerator for 30 minutes.

Heat the olive oil in a large, heavy-based frying pan. Add the meatballs in batches, and cook, stirring and turning frequently, until browned on all sides. Return earlier batches to the frying add the passata, chopped tomatoes and their can juices, vegetable stock and sugar, then on to taste with salt and pepper. Bring to the boil, reduce the heat, cover and simmer for 0 minutes, or until the sauce is thickened and the meatballs are tender and cooked through.

Meanwhile, bring a large, heavy-based saucepan of lightly salted water to the boil. Add the pasta, return to the boil and cook for 8–10 minutes, or until tender but still firm to the bite. and transfer to a warmed serving dish. Pour the sauce over the pasta and toss lightly. kle with the remaining parsley and serve immediately.

chilli con carne

££

- serves 4
- prepared in 15 mins
- cooks in 30 - 35 mins

2 tbsp sunflower oil
500 g/1 lb 2 oz fresh beef mince
1 large onion, chopped
1 garlic clove, finely chopped
1 green pepper, deseeded and
  diced
1 tsp chilli powder
800 g/1 lb 12 oz canned
  chopped tomatoes
800 g/1 lb 12 oz canned red
  kidney beans, drained and
  rinsed
450 ml/16 fl oz beef stock
salt
handful of fresh coriander sprigs
2 tbsp soured cream, to serve

1 Heat the oil in a large, heavy-based saucepan or flameproof casserole. Add the beef. Cook over a medium heat, stirring frequently, for 5 minutes, or until broken up and browned.

2 Reduce the heat, add the onion, garlic and pepper and cook, stirring frequently, for 10 minutes.

3 Stir in the chilli powder, tomatoes and their juices and kidney beans. Pour in the stock and season with salt. Bring to the boil,

reduce the heat and simmer, stirring frequently, for 15–20 minutes, or until the meat is tender.

4 Chop the coriander sprigs, reserving a few for a garnish, and stir into the chilli. Adjust the seasoning, if necessary. Either serve immediately with a splash of soured cream, and coriander sprigs to garnish, or leave to cool, then store in the refrigerator overnight. Reheating it the next day makes it more flavoursome.

2   3   4

carrot-topped beef pie

££

- serves 4
- prepared in 10 mins
- cooks in 1 hour 15 mins

450 g/1 lb lean minced beef
1 onion, chopped
1 garlic clove, crushed
1 tbsp plain flour
300 ml/10 fl oz beef stock
2 tbsp tomato purée
1 celery stick, chopped
3 tbsp chopped fresh parsley

1 tbsp Worcestershire sauce
675 g/1½ lb floury potatoes,
  diced
2 large carrots, diced
2 tbsp butter
3 tbsp skimmed milk
salt and pepper

1 Dry-fry the beef in a large pan set over a high heat for 3–4 minutes or until sealed. Add the onion and garlic and cook for a further 5 minutes, stirring.

2 Add the flour and cook for 1 minute. Gradually blend in the beef stock and tomato purée. Stir in the celery, 1 tablespoon of the parsley and the Worcestershire sauce. Season to taste.

3 Bring the mixture to the boil, then reduce the heat and simmer for 20–25 minutes. Spoon the beef mixture into a 1.2-litre/2-pint pie dish.

4 Meanwhile, cook the potatoes and carrots in a saucepan of boiling water for 10 minutes. Drain thoroughly and mash them together.

5 Stir the butter, milk and the remaining parsley into the potato and carrot mixture and season with salt and pepper to taste. Spoon the potato on top of the beef mixture to cover it completely; alternatively, pipe the potato over the top with a piping bag.

6 Cook the carrot-topped beef pie in a preheated oven, 190°C/375°F/Gas Mark 5, for 45 minutes or until cooked through. Serve piping hot.

shepherd's pie

££

- serves 4 - 5
- prepared in 10 mins
- cooks in 1½ hours

700 g/1 lb 9 oz lean minced or lamb or beef

2 onions, chopped

225 g/8 oz carrots, diced

1–2 garlic cloves, crushed

1 tbsp plain flour

200 ml/7 fl oz/beef stock

200 g/7 oz can chopped tomatoes

1 tsp Worcestershire sauce

1 tsp chopped fresh sage or oregano or ½ tsp dried sage or oregano

750 g–1 kg/1½–2 lb potatoes

25 g/1 oz/2 tbsp margarine

3–4 tbsp skimmed milk

125 g/4½ oz button mushrooms, sliced (optional)

salt and pepper

1 Place the meat in a heavy-based saucepan with no extra fat and cook gently, stirring frequently, until the meat begins to brown.

2 Add the onions, carrots and garlic and continue to cook gently for about 10 minutes. Stir in the flour and cook for a minute or so, then gradually stir in the stock and tomatoes and bring to the boil.

3 Add the Worcestershire sauce, seasoning and herbs, cover the pan and simmer gently for about 25 minutes, giving an occasional stir.

4 Cook the potatoes in boiling salted water until tender, then drain thoroughly and mash, beating in the margarine, seasoning and sufficient milk to give a piping consistency. Place in a piping bag fitted with a large star nozzle.

5 Stir the mushrooms (if using) into the meat and adjust the seasoning. Turn into a shallow ovenproof dish.

6 Pipe the potatoes evenly over the meat. Cook in a preheated oven at 200°C/400°F/Gas Mark 6 for about 30 minutes until piping hot and the potatoes are golden brown.

2

3

5

lamb & potato moussaka

- serves 4
- prepared in 45 mins
- cooks in 1¼ hours

1 large aubergine, sliced
1 tbsp olive or vegetable oil
1 onion, chopped finely
1 garlic clove, crushed
350 g/12 oz lean minced lamb
250 g/9 oz mushrooms, sliced
425 g/15 oz can chopped
  tomatoes with herbs
150 ml/¼ pint lamb or

vegetable stock
2 tbsp cornflour
2 tbsp water
500 g/1 lb 2 oz potatoes,
  parboiled for 10 minutes
  and sliced
2 eggs
125 g/4½ oz low-fat soft
  cheese

150 ml/¼ pint low-fat natural
  yogurt
60 g/2 oz grated low-fat
  mature Cheddar cheese
salt and pepper
fresh flat-leaf parsley,
  to garnish
green salad, to serve

1 Lay the aubergine slices on a clean surface and sprinkle liberally with salt, to extract the bitter juices. Leave for 10 minutes then turn the slices over and repeat. Put in a colander, rinse and drain well.

2 Meanwhile, heat the oil in a saucepan and fry the onion and garlic for 3–4 minutes. Add the lamb and mushrooms and cook for 5 minutes, until browned. Stir in the tomatoes and stock, bring to the boil and simmer for 10 minutes. Mix the cornflour with the water and stir into the pan. Cook, stirring, until thickened.

3 Spoon half the mixture into an ovenproof dish. Cover with the aubergine slices, then the remaining lamb mixture. Arrange the sliced potatoes on top.

4 Beat together the eggs, soft cheese, yogurt and seasoning. Pour over the potatoes to cover them completely. Sprinkle with the grated cheese.

5 Bake in a preheated oven at 190°C/375°F/Gas Mark 5 for 45 minutes until the topping is set and golden brown. Garnish with flat-leaf parsley and serve with a green salad.

pasticcio

££

- serves 4
- prepared in 15 mins
- cooks in 1 hour 40 mins

1 tbsp olive oil
1 onion, chopped
2 garlic cloves, finely
  chopped
450 g/1 lb fresh lamb mince
2 tbsp tomato purée

2 tbsp plain flour
300 ml/10 fl oz chicken
  stock (see page 9)
salt and pepper
1 tsp ground cinnamon
115 g/4 oz dried short-cut
  macaroni

2 beef tomatoes, sliced
300 ml/10 fl oz Greek yogurt
2 eggs, lightly beaten

1 Preheat the oven to 190°C/375°F/Gas Mark 5. Heat the olive oil in a large, heavy-based frying pan. Add the onion and garlic and cook over a low heat, stirring occasionally, for 5 minutes, or until softened. Add the lamb and cook, breaking it up with a wooden spoon, until browned all over. Add the tomato purée and sprinkle in the flour. Cook, stirring, for 1 minute, then stir in the chicken stock. Season to taste with salt and pepper and stir in the cinnamon. Bring to the boil, reduce the heat, cover and cook for 25 minutes.

1

2 Meanwhile, bring a large, heavy-based saucepan of lightly salted water to the boil. Add the pasta, return to the boil and cook for 8–10 minutes, or until tender but still firm to the bite.

2

3 Spoon the lamb mixture into a large ovenproof dish and arrange the tomato slices on top. Drain the pasta and transfer to a bowl. Add the yogurt and eggs and mix well. Spoon the pasta mixture on top of the lamb and bake in the preheated oven for 1 hour. Serve immediately.

3

pork hash

££

- serves 4
- prepared in 10 mins
- cooks in 55 mins

400 g/14 oz canned chopped
   tomatoes
600–700 ml/1–1¼ pints beef stock
1 tbsp sunflower oil
450 g/1 lb fresh pork mince
1 large onion, chopped
1 red pepper, deseeded and
   chopped
400 g/14 oz long-grain rice
1 tbsp chilli powder
450 g/1 lb fresh or frozen green
   beans salt and pepper

1 Preheat the oven to 180°C/ 350°F/Gas Mark 4. Drain the tomatoes, reserving their juices, and reserve. Make the juices up to 850 ml/1½ pints with the stock and reserve.

2 Heat the oil in a large, flameproof casserole. Add the pork, onion and red pepper and cook over a medium heat, stirring frequently, for 8–10 minutes, or until the onion is softened and the meat is broken up and golden brown. Add the rice and cook, stirring constantly, for 2 minutes.

3 Add the tomatoes, stock mixture, chilli powder and beans to the casserole and season to taste with salt and pepper. Bring to the boil, then cover and transfer to the preheated oven to bake for 40 minutes. Serve immediately.

1   2   3

chicken bake

££

- serves 4
- prepared in 45 mins, plus 1 hour cooling
- cooks in 40 mins

500 g/1 lb 2 oz minced chicken
1 large onion, finely chopped
2 carrots, finely diced
25 g/1 oz plain flour
1 tbsp tomato purée
300 ml/10 fl oz chicken stock
salt and pepper

pinch of fresh thyme
900 g/2 lb boiled potatoes,
  creamed with butter and milk
  and highly seasoned
85 g/3 oz grated Lancashire
  cheese
freshly cooked peas, to serve

2

1 Dry-fry the minced chicken, onion and carrots in a large, non-stick saucepan over a low heat, stirring frequently, for 5 minutes, or until the chicken has lost its pink colour. Sprinkle the chicken with the flour and cook, stirring constantly, for a further 2 minutes.

3

2 Gradually blend in the tomato purée and stock, then simmer for 15 minutes. Season to taste with salt and pepper and add the thyme.

3 Transfer the chicken and vegetable mixture to a large casserole and leave to cool completely.

4

4 Preheat the oven to 200°C/400°F/Gas Mark 6. Spoon the creamed potato over the chicken mixture and sprinkle with the Lancashire cheese. Bake in the preheated oven for 20 minutes, or until the cheese is bubbling and golden, then serve with freshly cooked peas.

chicken pepperonata

£££

- serves 4
- prepared in 15 mins
- cooks in 40 mins

8 chicken thighs
2 tbsp wholemeal flour
2 tbsp olive oil
1 small onion, thinly sliced
1 garlic clove, crushed
1 large red pepper, deseeded
   and thinly sliced
1 large yellow pepper, deseeded
   and thinly sliced
1 large green pepper. deseeded
   and thinly sliced
400 g/14 oz can chopped
   tomatoes
1 tbsp chopped fresh oregano
salt and pepper
fresh oregano, to garnish
crusty wholemeal bread,
   to serve

1 Remove the skin from the chicken thighs and toss the meat in the flour.

2 Heat the oil in a wide frying pan and fry the chicken over a medium heat until sealed and lightly browned, then remove from the pan.

3 Add the onion to the pan, lower the heat and cook, stirring occasionally, for about 5 minutes until softened, but not browned. Add the garlic, pepper slices, tomatoes and oregano, then bring to the boil, stirring constantly.

4 Arrange the chicken on top of the vegetables, season to taste with salt and pepper, then cover the pan tightly and simmer for 20–25 minutes or until the chicken is completely cooked and tender.

5 Taste and adjust the seasoning, if necessary. Transfer the chicken to a plate. Spoon the vegetables on to a warmed serving platter and top with the chicken. Garnish with oregano and serve immediately with crusty wholemeal bread.

1   2   4

jamaican hot pot

£££

- serves 4
- prepared in 5 mins
- cooks in 1¼ hours

2 tsp sunflower oil
4 chicken drumsticks
4 chicken thighs
1 medium onion
750 g/1 lb 10 oz piece
  squash or pumpkin, peeled
1 green pepper

2.5 cm/1 inch fresh ginger
  root, chopped finely
425 g/15 oz can chopped
  tomatoes
300ml/½ pint chicken stock
60 g/2 oz split lentils
garlic salt and cayenne pepper
350 g/12 oz can sweetcorn

1 Heat the oil in a large flameproof casserole and fry the chicken joints, turning frequently, until they are golden all over.

2 Peel and slice the onion.

3 Using a sharp knife, cut the squash or pumpkin into dice.

4 Deseed and slice the green pepper.

2

3

4

5 Drain any excess fat from the pan and add the onion, pumpkin and pepper. Gently fry for a few minutes. Add the ginger, tomatoes, stock and lentils. Season with garlic salt and cayenne.

6 Cover and place in a preheated oven, 190°C/375°F/Gas Mark 5, for about 1 hour, until the vegetables are tender and the juices from the chicken run clear.

7 Add the drained corn and cook for a further 5 minutes. Season to taste and serve with crusty bread.

minty lime chicken

££

- serves 6
- prepared in 35 mins, plus 30 mins marinating
- cooks in 20 mins

**3 tbsp finely chopped fresh
    mint**
4 tbsp clear honey
4 tbsp lime juice
salt and pepper
12 boneless chicken thighs
mixed salad, to serve

SAUCE
**150 g/5½ oz low-fat natural
    thick yogurt**
**1 tbsp finely chopped fresh
    mint**
2 tsp finely grated lime rind

1 Mix the mint, honey and lime juice in a large bowl and season to taste with salt and pepper. Use cocktail sticks to keep the chicken thighs in neat shapes and add the chicken to the marinade, turning to coat evenly.

2 Cover with clingfilm and leave the chicken to marinate in the refrigerator for at least 30 minutes, longer if possible. Remove the chicken from the marinade and drain. Reserve the marinade.

1

3 Preheat the grill to medium. Place the chicken on a grill rack and cook under the hot grill for 15–18 minutes, or until the chicken is tender and the juices run clear when a skewer is inserted into the thickest part of the meat. Turn the chicken frequently and baste with the marinade. Alternatively, cook over hot coals on a lit barbecue.

1

4 Meanwhile, mix all the sauce ingredients together in a bowl. Remove the cocktail sticks and serve the chicken with a salad and the sauce for dipping.

4

macaroni & tuna fish layer

££

- serves 4
- prepared in 20 mins
- cooks in 50 mins

300 g/11 oz dried macaroni

3 tbsp olive oil

1 garlic clove, crushed

100 g/3½ oz button mushrooms, sliced

1 red pepper, thinly sliced

400 g/14 oz canned tuna in brine, drained and flaked

1 tsp dried oregano

salt and pepper

SAUCE

50 g/2 oz butter or margarine, plus extra for greasing

2 tbsp plain flour

500 g/16 fl oz milk

3 tomatoes, sliced

4 tbsp dried breadcrumbs

50 g/2 oz mature Cheddar or Parmesan cheese, grated

1 Preheat the oven to 200°C/400°F/Gas Mark 6. Bring a large saucepan of lightly salted water to the boil. Add the macaroni, return to the boil and cook for 10–12 minutes, or until tender but still firm to the bite. Drain, rinse and drain thoroughly.

2 Heat the olive oil in a frying pan and fry the garlic, mushrooms and pepper until soft. Add the tuna, oregano and add salt and pepper to taste. Heat through. Grease a 1-litre/1¾-pint ovenproof dish with a little butter or margarine. Add half of the cooked macaroni, cover with the tuna mixture, then add the remaining macaroni.

3 To make the sauce, melt the butter or margarine in a saucepan, stir in the flour and cook for 1 minute. Add the milk gradually and bring to the boil. Simmer for 1–2 minutes, stirring constantly, until thickened. Season to taste with salt and pepper. Pour the sauce over the macaroni. Lay the sliced tomatoes over the sauce and sprinkle with the breadcrumbs and cheese. Cook in the preheated oven for 25 minutes, or until piping hot and the top is well browned.

2   3   3

NOTE: If you invest in a block of fresh Parmesan it can be stored in the fridge for a long period and thus becomes an economical ingredient.

smoked fish lasagne

£££

- serves 4
- prepared in 20 mins
- cooks in 1½ hours

2 tsp olive or vegetable oil
1 garlic clove, crushed
1 small onion, chopped finely
125 g/4½ oz mushrooms, sliced
400 g/14 oz can chopped
   tomatoes
1 small courgette, sliced
150 ml/¼ pint vegetable stock
   or water
25 g/1 oz butter or margarine
300 ml/½ pint skimmed milk
25 g/1 oz plain flour

125 g/4 oz grated mature
   Cheddar cheese
1 tbsp chopped fresh parsley
125 g/4½ oz (6 sheets) pre-
   cooked lasagne
350 g/12 oz skinned and boned
   smoked cod or haddock, cut
   into chunks
salt and pepper
fresh parsley sprigs to garnish

1

2

4

1 Heat the oil in a saucepan and fry the garlic and onion for about 5 minutes. Add the mushrooms and cook for 3 minutes, stirring.

2 Add the tomatoes, courgette and stock or water and simmer, uncovered, for 15–20 minutes until the vegetables are soft. Season.

3 Put the butter or margarine, milk and flour into a small saucepan and heat, whisking constantly, until the sauce boils and thickens. Remove from the heat and add half of the cheese and all of the parsley. Stir gently to melt the cheese and season to taste.

4 Spoon the tomato sauce mixture into a large, shallow ovenproof dish and top with half of the lasagne sheets. Scatter the chunks of fish evenly over the top, then pour over half of the cheese sauce. Top with the remaining lasagne sheets and then spread the rest of the cheese sauce on top. Sprinkle with the remaining cheese.

5 Bake in a preheated oven at 190°C/375°F/Gas Mark 5 for 40 minutes, until the top is golden brown and bubbling. Garnish with parsley sprigs and serve hot.

spaghetti alla puttanesca

££

- serves 4
- prepared in 10 mins
- cooks in 35 - 40 mins

3 tbsp olive oil

2 garlic cloves, finely chopped

10 canned anchovy fillets,
drained and chopped

140 g/5 oz black olives, stoned
and chopped

1 tbsp capers, drained and
rinsed

450 g/1 lb plum tomatoes,
peeled, deseeded and chopped

pinch of cayenne pepper, salt

400 g/14 oz dried spaghetti

2 tbsp chopped fresh parsley,
to garnish (optional)

1 Heat the olive oil in a heavy-based frying pan. Add the garlic and cook over a low heat, stirring frequently, for 2 minutes. Add the anchovies and mash them to a pulp with a fork. Add the olives, capers and tomatoes and season to taste with cayenne pepper. Cover and simmer for 25 minutes.

2 Meanwhile, bring a large, heavy-based saucepan of lightly salted water to the boil. Add the pasta, return to the boil and cook for 8–10 minutes, or until tender but still firm to the bite. Drain well and transfer to a warmed serving dish.

3 Spoon the anchovy sauce into the dish and toss the pasta, using 2 large forks. Garnish with the chopped parsley, if using, and serve immediately.

1   2   3

spaghettini with quick tuna sauce

££

- serves 4
- prepared in 20 mins
- cooks in 30 mins

3 tbsp olive oil

4 tomatoes, peeled, deseeded and roughly chopped

115 g/4 oz mushrooms, sliced

1 tbsp shredded fresh basil

400 g/14 oz canned tuna, drained

100 ml/3½ fl oz fish stock

1 garlic clove, finely chopped

2 tsp chopped fresh marjoram

salt and pepper

350 g/12 oz dried spaghettini

115 g/4 oz freshly grated Parmesan cheese, to serve

1 Heat the olive oil in a large frying pan. Add the tomatoes and cook over low heat, stirring occasionally, for 15 minutes, or until pulpy. Add the mushrooms and cook, stirring occasionally, for an additional 10 minutes. Stir in the basil, tuna, fish stock, garlic, and marjoram, and season to taste with salt and pepper. Cook over low heat for 5 minutes, or until heated through.

2 Meanwhile, bring a large heavy-bottom pan of lightly salted water to a boil. Add the pasta, return to a boil, and cook for 8–10 minutes, or until tender but still firm to the bite.

3 Drain the pasta well, transfer to a warmed serving dish, and spoon on the tuna mixture. Serve with grated Parmesan cheese.

NOTE: If you invest in a block of fresh Parmesan it can be stored in the fridge for a long period and thus becomes an economical ingredient

potato & vegetable curry

■ serves 4
■ prepared in 5 mins
■ cooks in 45 mins

4 tbsp vegetable oil
675 g/1 lb 8 oz waxy
   potatoes, cut into large
   chunks
2 onions, quartered
3 garlic cloves, crushed
1 tsp garam masala
½ tsp ground turmeric
½ tsp ground cumin

½ tsp ground coriander
2 tsp grated fresh root
   ginger
1 fresh red chilli, chopped
225 g/8 oz cauliflower
   florets
4 tomatoes, peeled and
   quartered
75 g/2¾ oz frozen peas

2 tbsp chopped fresh
   coriander
300 ml/10 fl oz vegetable
   stock
shredded fresh coriander,
   to garnish
boiled rice or warm Indian
   bread, to serve

1 Heat the vegetable oil in a large heavy-based saucepan or frying pan. Add the potato chunks, onions and garlic and fry over a low heat, stirring frequently, for 2–3 minutes.

2 Add the garam masala, turmeric, ground cumin, ground coriander, ginger and chilli to the pan, mixing the spices into the vegetables until they are well coated. Fry over a low heat, stirring constantly, for 1 minute.

1

3 Add the cauliflower florets, tomatoes, peas, chopped fresh coriander and vegetable stock to the curry mixture.

4 Cook the potato curry over a low heat for 30–40 minutes or until the potatoes are tender and completely cooked through.

2

5 Garnish the potato curry with fresh coriander and serve with plain boiled rice or warm Indian bread.

3

vegetable enchiladas

££

- serves 4
- prepared in 20 mins
- cooks in 55 mins

4 flour tortillas
75 g/2¾ oz grated
  Cheddar cheese
FILLING
75 g/2¾ oz spinach
2 tbsp olive oil
8 baby corn cobs, sliced
25 g/1 oz frozen peas, thawed
1 red pepper, seeded and diced
1 carrot, diced
1 leek, sliced
2 garlic cloves, crushed
1 red chilli, chopped
salt and pepper
SAUCE
300 ml/½ pint passata
2 shallots, chopped
1 garlic clove, crushed
300 ml/½ pint vegetable stock
1 tsp caster sugar
1 tsp chilli powder

1 To make the filling, blanch the spinach in a pan of boiling water for 2 minutes. Drain well, pressing out as much excess moisture as possible, and chop.

2 Heat the oil in a frying pan over a medium heat. Add the baby corn cobs, peas, pepper, carrot, leek, garlic and chilli and sauté, stirring briskly, for 3–4 minutes. Stir in the spinach and season well with salt and pepper to taste.

3 Put all the sauce ingredients in a heavy-based saucepan and bring to the boil, stirring constantly. Cook over a high heat, stirring constantly, for 20 minutes, until thickened and reduced by a third.

4 Spoon a quarter of the filling along the centre of each tortilla. Roll the tortillas around the filling and place, seam side down, in a single layer in an ovenproof dish.

5 Pour the sauce over the tortillas and sprinkle the cheese on top. Cook in a preheated oven, 180°C/ 350°F/ Gas Mark 4, for 20 minutes, or until the cheese has melted and browned. Serve immediately.

2   4   4

tomato, mushroom & macaroni hot pot

£

- serves 4
- prepared in 20 mins
- cooks in 30 mins

3 tbsp olive oil

1 onion, sliced

75 g/2¾ oz mushrooms,
  sliced thinly

2 garlic cloves, chopped
  very finely

1 tsp dried oregano

2 tbsp tomato purée

3 tbsp chopped fresh
  flat-leaf parsley

800 g/1lb 12 oz canned
  chopped tomatoes

450 ml/16 fl oz chicken stock

225 g/8 oz dried short macaroni

1 tsp salt

¼ tsp pepper

freshly grated
  Parmesan, to serve

1 Heat the olive oil in a large saucepan or high-sided frying pan with a lid, over medium heat. Add the onion and mushrooms. Cook, stirring for 5–7 minutes, or until soft.

2 Stir in the garlic, oregano, tomato purée and 1½ tablespoons of the parsley. Cook for 1 minute. Pour in the tomatoes and stock. Bring to the boil.

3 Add the macaroni, salt and pepper. Bring back to the boil. Cover and simmer over a medium–low heat for 20 minutes, stirring occasionally, or until the macaroni is tender.

4 Sprinkle with the remaining parsley just before serving. Serve with freshly grated Parmesan.

NOTE: If you invest in a block of fresh Parmesan it can be stored in the fridge for a long period and thus becomes an economical ingredient

cold weather casserole

££

- serves 6
- prepared in 20 mins
- cooks in 1 hour 15 mins

55 g/2 oz butter or
vegan margarine
2 leeks, sliced
2 carrots, sliced
2 potatoes, cut into bite-sized
pieces
1 swede, cut into bite-sized
pieces
2 courgettes, sliced
1 fennel bulb, halved and sliced
2 tbsp plain flour
425 g/15 oz canned butter
beans
600 ml/1 pint vegetable stock
2 tbsp tomato purée
1 tsp dried thyme
2 bay leaves
salt and pepper
DUMPLINGS
115 g/4 oz self-raising flour
pinch of salt
55 g/2 oz vegetarian suet
2 tbsp chopped fresh parsley
about 4 tbsp water

1 Melt the butter in a large, heavy-based saucepan over a low heat. Add the leeks, carrots, potatoes, swede, courgettes and fennel and cook, stirring occasionally, for 10 minutes. Stir in the flour and cook, stirring constantly, for 1 minute. Stir in the can juice from the beans, the stock, tomato purée, thyme and bay leaves and season to taste with salt and pepper. Bring to the boil, stirring constantly, then cover and simmer for 10 minutes.

2 Meanwhile, make the dumplings. Sift the flour and salt into a bowl. Stir in the suet and parsley, then add enough water to bind to a soft dough. Divide the dough into 8 pieces and roll into balls.

3 Add the butter beans and dumplings to the saucepan, cover and simmer for a further 30 minutes. Remove and discard the bay leaf before serving.

1   2   3

chickpea hot pot

£

- serves 4
- prepared in 15 mins
- cooks in 2 hours 30 mins

225 g/8 oz dried chickpeas,
   soaked overnight in enough
   water to cover
3 tbsp olive oil
1 large onion, sliced
2 garlic cloves, finely chopped
2 leeks, sliced
175 g/6 oz carrots, sliced

4 turnips, sliced
4 celery sticks, sliced
115 g/4 oz bulgar wheat
400 g/14 oz canned chopped
   tomatoes
2 tbsp snipped fresh chives,
   plus extra to garnish
salt and pepper

1 Drain the chickpeas and place in a heavy-based saucepan. Add enough water to cover, bring to the boil and simmer for 1¹/₂ hours.

2 Meanwhile, heat the oil in a large saucepan. Add the sliced onion and cook, stirring, for 5 minutes, or until softened. Add the garlic, leeks, carrots, turnips and celery and cook, stirring occasionally, for 5 minutes. Stir in the bulgar wheat, tomatoes and chives, season to taste with salt and pepper and bring to the boil. Spoon the mixture into a heatproof pudding basin, cover with a lid of foil and reserve.

1

3 When the chickpeas have been cooking for 1¹/₂ hours, set a steamer over the saucepan. Place the basin inside the steamer, cover tightly and cook for a further 40 minutes. Remove the basin from the steamer, drain the chickpeas, then stir them into the vegetable and bulgar wheat mixture. Transfer to a warmed serving dish and serve immediately, garnished with extra chives.

2

3

vegetable crumble

- serves 4
- prepared in 15 mins
- cooks in 40 mins

1 cauliflower, cut into florets
salt and pepper
2 tbsp sunflower oil
25 g/1 oz plain flour
350 ml/12 fl oz milk
325 g/11½ oz canned
  sweetcorn kernels, drained
2 tbsp chopped fresh parsley
1 tsp chopped fresh thyme
140 g/5 oz Cheddar cheese,
  grated
TOPPING
55 g/2 oz wholemeal flour
25 g/1 oz butter
25 g/1 oz rolled oats
25 g/1 oz blanched almonds,
  chopped

1 Preheat the oven to 190°C/ 375°F/Gas Mark 5. Cook the cauliflower in a saucepan of lightly salted boiling water for 5 minutes. Drain well, reserving the cooking water. Heat the oil in a saucepan and stir in the flour. Cook, stirring constantly, for 1 minute. Remove the saucepan from the heat and gradually stir in the milk and 150 ml/5 fl oz of the reserved cooking water. Return the saucepan to the heat and bring to the boil, stirring constantly. Cook, stirring, for 3 minutes, or until thickened. Remove the saucepan from the heat.

2 Stir the sweetcorn, parsley, thyme and half the cheese into the sauce and season to taste with salt and pepper. Fold in the cauliflower, then spoon the mixture into an ovenproof dish.

3 To make the crumble topping, place the flour in a bowl, add the butter and rub it in with your fingertips until the mixture resembles breadcrumbs. Stir in the oats and almonds, add the remaining cheese, then sprinkle the mixture evenly over the vegetables. Bake in the preheated oven for 30 minutes. Serve immediately.

1   2   3

vegetable & lentil casserole

■ serves 4
■ prepared in 15 mins
■ cooks in 2 hours

1 onion
4 cloves
225 g/8 oz Puy or green lentils
1 bay leaf
1.5 litres/2¾ pints vegetable
  stock or water
2 leeks, sliced
2 potatoes, diced

2 carrots, chopped
3 courgettes, sliced
1 celery stick, chopped
1 red pepper, deseeded and
  chopped
salt and pepper
1 tbsp lemon juice

1

1 Stick the onion with the cloves. Put the lentils in a large casserole, add the onion and bay leaf and pour in the vegetable stock or water. Cover and bake in a preheated oven, 180°C/350°F/ Gas Mark 4, for 1 hour.

1

2 Remove the casserole from the oven. Take out the onion and discard the cloves. Slice the onion and return it to the casserole with the leeks, potatoes, carrots, courgettes, celery and red pepper. Stir thoroughly and season to taste with salt and pepper. Cover and return to the oven for a further hour.

2

3 Remove and discard the bay leaf. Stir the lemon juice into the casserole and serve immediately, straight from the dish.

desserts

Forget over-processed, costly and unsatisfying pots of yogurt and frozen desserts and rediscover traditional - and economical - favourites such as Chocolate Fudge Pudding, Traditional Apple Pie and Fruit Brûlée. You'll notice the difference in the smiles on the family's faces and the extra change in your purse.

chocolate fudge pudding

££

- serves 6
- prepared in 10 mins
- cooks in 35 - 40 mins

150 g/5½ oz soft margarine

150 g/5½ oz self-raising flour

150 g/5½ oz golden syrup

3 eggs

25 g/1 oz cocoa powder

CHOCOLATE FUDGE SAUCE

100 g/3½ oz dark chocolate

125 ml/4 fl oz condensed milk

4 tbsp double cream

1 Lightly grease a 1.2 litre/2 pint pudding basin.

2 Place the ingredients for the sponge in a mixing bowl and beat until well combined and smooth.

3 Spoon into the prepared basin and level the top. Cover with a disc of baking paper and tie a pleated sheet of foil over the basin. Steam the pudding for 1½–2 hours until it is cooked through and springy to the touch.

4 To make the chocolate fudge sauce, break the chocolate

into small pieces and place them in a small pan with the condensed milk. Heat gently, stirring, until the chocolate melts.

5 Remove the pan from the heat and stir in the double cream.

6 To serve the pudding, turn it out on to a warm serving plate and pour over a little of the chocolate fudge sauce to decorate. Serve the pudding warm, with the remaining sauce.

2

3

5

queen of puddings

- serves 8
- prepared in 15 mins, plus 15 mins standing
- cooks in 50 mins

2 tbsp butter, plus extra
  for greasing
600 ml/1 pint milk
225 g/8 oz caster sugar
finely grated rind
  of 1 orange
4 eggs, separated
75 g/2¾ oz fresh

breadcrumbs
salt
6 tbsp orange marmalade

1 Grease a 1.5-litre/2³/₄-pint ovenproof dish with butter.

2 To make the custard, heat the milk in a saucepan with the butter, 50 g/1³/₄ oz of the caster sugar and the grated orange rind until just warm.

3 Whisk the egg yolks in a bowl. Gradually pour the warm milk over the eggs, whisking constantly. Stir the breadcrumbs into the bowl, then transfer the mixture to the dish and leave to stand for 15 minutes.

4 Preheat the oven to 180°C/350°F/Gas Mark 4,then bake the pudding for 20–25 minutes, until the custard has just set. Remove the custard from the oven but do not turn the oven off.

5 To make the meringue, whisk the egg whites with a pinch of salt in a spotlessly clean, greasefree bowl until soft peaks form. Whisk in the remaining sugar, a little at a time. Spread the orange marmalade over the cooked custard. Top with the meringue, spreading it right to the edges of the dish. Return the pudding to the oven and bake for a further 20 minutes, or until the meringue is crisp and golden.

bread & butter pudding

- serves 4
- prepared in 15 mins
- cooks in 40

6 medium slices of day-old wholemeal bread, crusts removed
2 tbsp butter
2 tbsp sugar
25 g/1 oz sultanas
25 g/1 oz currants
425 ml/15 fl oz milk

2 eggs
½ tsp ground mixed spice

1 Preheat the oven to 180°C/350°F/Gas Mark 4. Spread the slices of bread with butter, then cut each slice into quarters. Arrange half of the bread, buttered side up, on the bottom of an 850-ml/1½-pint ovenproof dish. Sprinkle over half of the sugar, then scatter over half of the sultanas and currants. Top with the remaining bread, then sprinkle over the remaining sugar and fruit.

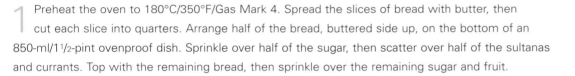
1

2 Pour the milk into a large mixing bowl. Add the eggs and mixed spice and whisk until smooth. Pour the mixture evenly over the bread, then transfer to the preheated oven and bake for about 40 minutes. Remove from the oven and serve hot.

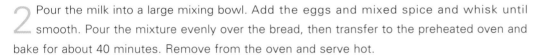

1

1

1

traditional apple pie

- serves 6
- prepared in 50 mins
- cooks in 55 mins

750 g–1 kg/1 lb 10 oz–2 lb 4 oz
Bramley apples, peeled, cored
and sliced
about 125 g/4½ oz brown
or white sugar, plus extra
for sprinkling
½–1 tsp ground cinnamon,
mixed spice or ground ginger
1–2 tbsp water
SHORTCRUST PASTRY
350 g/12 oz plain flour
pinch of salt
90 g/3 oz butter or margarine
90 g/3 oz white vegetable fat
about 6 tbsp cold water
beaten egg or milk, for glazing

1 To make the pastry, sift the plain flour and salt into a large mixing bowl. Add the butter or margarine and white vegetable fat and rub in with the fingertips until the mixture resembles fine breadcrumbs. Add the water to the mixture and gather the ingredients together into a dough. Wrap the dough in kitchen foil and chill for around 30 minutes.

2 Roll out almost two-thirds of the pastry thinly and use it to line a 20–23 cm/8–9 inch deep pie plate or shallow pie tin.

3 Mix the cooking apples with the brown or white sugar and spice in a mixing bowl and pack into the pastry case; the filling can come up above the rim of the pastry in the pie plate. Add the water if liked, particularly if the cooking apples are a dry variety.

4 Roll out the remaining pastry to form a lid for the pie. Dampen the edges of the pie rim with water and position the lid, pressing the edges firmly together with your fingers. Trim the edges and crimp them decoratively.

5 Use the trimmings to cut out leaves or other shapes to decorate the top of the pie, dampen and attach. Glaze the top of the pie with beaten egg or milk, make 1–2 slits in the top and put the pie on a baking sheet.

6 Bake in a preheated oven, 220°C/425°F/Gas Mark 7, for 20 minutes, then reduce the temperature to 180°C/350°F/Gas Mark 4 and cook for about 30 minutes, until the pastry is a light golden brown. Serve the pie hot or cold, sprinkled with sugar.

3   4   5

fruit brûlée

££

- serves 4
- prepared in 15 mins
- cooks in 1¼ hour

4 plums, stoned and sliced
2 cooking apples, peeled and sliced
1 tsp ground ginger
600 ml/1 pint Greek-style yogurt
2 tbsp icing sugar, sifted
1 tsp almond essence
85 g/3 oz demerara sugar

2

1 Put the plums and apples in a pan with 2 tablespoons of water and cook for 7–10 minutes, until tender, but not mushy. Set aside to cool, then stir in the ground ginger.

2 Using a draining spoon, spoon the mixture into the base of a shallow, heatproof serving dish.

3

3 Combine the yogurt, icing sugar and almond essence and spoon on to the fruit to cover.

4 Sprinkle the demerara sugar over the top of the yogurt and cook under a hot grill for 3–4 minutes or until the sugar has melted and formed a crust.

4

5 Set aside to chill in the refrigerator for 1 hour before serving.

lemon meringue pie

££

- serves 4
- prepared in 20+30 mins
- cooks in 1 hour

PASTRY

200 g/7 oz plain flour, plus

   extra for dusting

100 g/3½ oz butter, diced, plus

   extra for greasing

50 g/1¾ oz icing sugar, sifted

finely grated rind of 1 lemon

1 egg yolk, beaten

3 tbsp milk

FILLING

3 tbsp cornflour

300 ml/10 fl oz cold water

juice and grated rind of 2 lemons

175 g/6 oz caster sugar

2 eggs, separated

1 To make the pastry, sift the flour into a bowl and rub in the butter. Mix in the remaining ingredients. Knead briefly on a lightly floured work surface. Leave to rest for 30 minutes. Preheat the oven to 180°C/350°F/Gas Mark 4. Grease a 20-cm/8-inch ovenproof pie dish with butter. Roll out the pastry to a thickness of 5 mm/¼ inch and use it to line the dish. Prick with a fork, line with baking paper and fill with baking beans. Bake for 15 minutes. Remove from the oven. Lower the temperature to 150°C/300°F/Gas Mark 2.

2 To make the filling, mix the cornflour with a little water. Put the remaining water into a pan. Stir in the lemon juice and rind and cornflour paste. Bring to the boil, stirring. Cook for 2 minutes. Cool a little. Stir in 5 tablespoons of sugar and the egg yolks and pour into the pastry shell. In a separate bowl, whisk the egg whites until stiff. Gradually whisk in the remaining sugar and spread over the pie. Bake for 40 minutes. Remove from the oven and serve.

2

2

2

pear cake

■ serves 12
■ prepared in 25 mins
■ cooks in 1½ hours

margarine, for greasing
4 pears, peeled and cored
2 tbsp water
200 g/7 oz plain flour
2 tsp baking powder
100 g/3½ oz soft light
  brown sugar

4 tbsp milk
2 tbsp clear honey, plus
  extra for drizzling
2 tsp ground cinnamon
2 egg whites

1 Grease and line the base of a 20 cm/8 inch cake tin.

2 Put 1 pear in a food processor with the water and process until almost smooth. Transfer to a mixing bowl.

3 Sift in the flour and baking powder. Beat in the sugar, milk, honey and cinnamon and mix well.

4 Chop all but 1 of the remaining pears and add to the mixture.

5 Whisk the egg whites until peaks form and gently fold into the mixture until fully blended.

6 Slice the remaining pear and arrange it in a fan pattern on the base of the prepared tin.

7 Spoon the cake mixture into the tin and cook in a preheated oven, 150°C/300°F/Gas Mark 2, for 1¼ –1½ hours or until cooked through.

8 Remove the cake from the oven and set aside to cool in the tin for 10 minutes. Turn the cake out on to a wire cooling rack and drizzle with honey. Set aside to cool completely, then cut into slices to serve.

chocolate fruit crumble

£££

- serves 4
- prepared in 10 mins
- cooks in 40 - 45 mins

6 tbsp butter, plus extra for
  greasing
400 g/14 oz canned apricots,
  in natural juice
450 g/1 lb cooking apples,
  peeled and thickly sliced
100 g/3½ oz plain flour

50 g/1¾ oz porridge oats
4 tbsp caster sugar
100 g/3½ oz chocolate chips

1 Preheat the oven to 350°F/180°C/Gas Mark 4. Grease an ovenproof dish with
a little butter.

2 Drain the apricots, reserving 4 tablespoons of the juice. Place the apples and apricots in the
prepared ovenproof dish with the reserved apricot juice and toss to mix thoroughly.

2

3 Sift the flour into a large bowl. Cut the butter into small cubes and rub it in with your fingertips
until the mixture resembles fine breadcrumbs. Stir in the porridge oats, caster sugar and
chocolate chips.

3

4 Sprinkle the crumble mixture over the apples and apricots and smooth the top roughly. Do not
press the crumble down on to the fruit. Bake in the preheated oven for 40–45 minutes, or until
the topping is golden. Serve the crumble hot or cold.

4

index

beans and pulses
chickpea hot pot 77
chilli beans 32
chilli con carne 46
cold weather casserole 74
Jamaican hot pot 60
mushroom and bean chilli 76
vegetable and lentil casserole 80
beef
beef in beer with herb dumplings 42
beef and tomato gratin 44
carrot-topped beef pie 48
chilli con carne 46
shepherd's pie 50
spaghetti bolognese 40
spaghetti and meatballs 45

cabbage: bubble and squeak 28
carrots
carrot and cumin soup 18
carrot-topped beef pie 48
cauliflower
potato and vegetable curry 69
vegetable crumble 78
cheese
beef and tomato gratin 44
bread and butter savoury 30
cheese and potato slices 26
cheesy vegetable chowder 16
chicken bake 56
lamb and potato moussaka 52
macaroni and tuna fish layer 62
potato crumble 20
smoked fish lasagne 64
vegetable crumble 78
vegetable enchiladas 70
chicken
chicken bake 56
chicken pepperonata 58
chicken stock 9
cream of chicken soup 14
Jamaican hot pot 60
minty lime chicken 61
chillies
chilli beans 32
chilli con carne 46
mushroom and bean chilli 76
pork hash 54
potato and vegetable curry 69
vegetable enchiladas 70
chocolate
chocolate fruit crumble 95
chocolate fudge pudding 84
courgettes
beef and tomato gratin 44
cold weather casserole 74

crispy vegetable pancakes 35
vegetable and lentil casserole 80

eggs
bread and butter pudding 87
bread and butter savoury 30
cheese and potato slices 26
crispy vegetable pancakes 35
lamb and potato moussaka 52
pasticcio 53
queen of puddings 86
Spanish potato omelette 24
tomato and onion bake 22

fish: smoked fish lasagne 64
fruit
apple pie 88
chocolate fruit crumble 95
fruit brûlée 90
lemon meringue pie 92
pear cake 94

lamb
lamb and potato moussaka 52
pasticcio 53
shepherd's pie 50
liver: pan-fried liver and bacon with potato
cakes 27

mushrooms
lamb and potato moussaka 52
macaroni and tuna fish layer 62
mushroom and bean chilli 76
smoked fish lasagne 64
spaghettini with quick tuna sauce 68
tomato, mushroom and macaroni hot pot 72

pasta
macaroni and tuna fish layer 62
pasticcio 53
smoked fish lasagne 64
spaghetti alla puttanesca 66
spaghetti bolognese 40
spaghetti and meatballs 45
spaghettini with quick tuna sauce 68
tomato, mushroom and macaroni hot pot 72
peas
pea and ham soup 19
potato and vegetable curry 69
vegetable enchiladas 70
peppers
chicken pepperonata 58
chilli con carne 46
Jamaican hot pot 60
macaroni and tuna fish layer 62
mushroom and bean chilli 76

pork hash 54
vegetable enchiladas 70
vegetable and lentil casserole 80
pork hash 54
potatoes
bubble and squeak 28
carrot-topped beef pie 48
cheese and potato slices 26
chicken bake 56
cold weather casserole 74
crispy vegetable pancakes 35
herby potatoes and onion 36
lamb and potato moussaka 52
pan-fried liver and bacon with potato
cakes 27
paprika potatoes 34
potato crumble 20
potato and vegetable curry 69
shepherd's pie 50
Spanish potato omelette 24
vegetable and lentil casserole 80

sweetcorn
Jamaican hot pot 60
vegetable crumble 78
vegetable enchiladas 70

tomatoes
beef and tomato gratin 44
chicken pepperonata 58
chickpea hot pot 77
chilli beans 32
chilli con carne 46
Jamaican hot pot 60
lamb and potato moussaka 52
mushroom and bean chilli 76
pasticcio 53
pork hash 54
potato and vegetable curry 69
shepherd's pie 50
smoked fish lasagne 64
spaghetti alla puttanesca 66
spaghetti bolognese 40
spaghetti and meatballs 45
spaghettini with quick tuna sauce 68
tomato, mushroom and macaroni hot pot 72
tomato and onion bake 22
tomato soup 12
tuna
macaroni and tuna fish layer 62
spaghettini with quick tuna sauce 68